URBAN
PROCESSES

as viewed by the social sciences

A National Academy of Sciences Symposium
Organized by The Urban Institute
Moderated by William Gorham

URBAN PROCESSES

as viewed by the social sciences

Kenneth J. Arrow
James G. March
James S. Coleman
Anthony Downs

THE URBAN INSTITUTE

Washington, D. C.

SBN No. 87766-001-8
Library of Congress Catalog Card No. 73-120085
UI 5-301-4

Available from:

Publications Office
The Urban Institute
2100 M Street, N.W.
Washington, D. C. 20037

List price: $1.95

Printed in the United States of America

Table of Contents

Introduction:

Need for a New Understanding

William Gorham

Increasingly, astute observers of the urban scene are concluding that the most intractable and, alas, the most important and threatening aspects of our urban problems are rooted not in our wealth or in the programs we mount to combat the problems, but in our institutions and the processes of our society.

Until the early 1960's, the comfortable assumption of many was that if we directed more public resources to particular problems we could readily solve them. Now we are finding—as we look at black-white tensions, or alienation, or maldistribution of income—that this is not necessarily true. For some decades we have been providing the money and manpower to deal with the problems, for instance, of education and transportation. We put these inputs, figuratively, into a little box, representing our society and its processes—trusting that the desired results would pop out the other side. Well, they did not. The outputs have been less than we expected. The disappointment and the puzzlement over where to turn is a great deal of what confrontations, citizen participation,

black power, and the rest of the things that most people regard as
the crisis of the cities is all about. We recognize now that we need
new understanding.

In this symposium, organized by The Urban Institute for the
National Academy of Sciences, instead of focusing on special
programs for the cities, we will concentrate on the institutions
which distribute wealth and power in our society. The larger public
looks for guidance in the quest for understanding to the social
scientist who has traditionally grasped the issues of institutions and
processes as central. Therefore, representatives of three social
science disciplines—economics, political science, and sociology—
will seek to throw light on complex urban problems from their
own perspectives in the discussion that follows.

Kenneth J. Arrow, professor of economics at Harvard University,
focuses on the price system and the market as the principal engines
of urban growth and of the satisfaction of demands. While describ-
ing the price system as a useful and generally successful engine, he
underscores the fact that it has nevertheless major limitations
as well.

James G. March, political scientist and dean of the School of
Social Science at the University of California at Irvine, analyzes
how the political system tries to compensate for the inadequacies
of the price system in allocating both wealth and power. He touches
on the potentials of the political system and explains how and why
and under what conditions this system, like the price system, also
may fail.

James S. Coleman, professor of sociology at Johns Hopkins
University, outlines some of the social preconditions for the more
or less successful functioning of the economic and political institutions. He explores the conditions under which society, or a part of
society, withdraws its support, denies the legitimacy of institutions,
and at times even resorts to violence to seek its ends when it
feels that it cannot otherwise achieve them.

Anthony Downs, economist and chief executive officer of the Real Estate Research Corporation, brings together the insights of the three disciplines—economics, political science and sociology—to analyze a crucial question for cities and for the nation: the future of the urban ghetto.

URBAN
PROCESSES

as viewed by the social sciences

The Effects of the Price System and Market on Urban Economic Development

Kenneth J. Arrow

The predominant mode by which we make decisions that shape our daily lives is through the operation of the private market and the price system. The goods we consume, the houses we buy and the work we choose are all mediated by purchases and sales. Individuals derive their income by selling personal services or services resulting from things they own at given prices. They use this income to purchase goods, again at given prices.

THE "EFFICIENT" ALLOCATION OF RESOURCES

It is a theorem that if society's demands and supplies are consistent with each other (that is, society is producing neither more nor less than people want at these prices), then the resulting state is efficient—providing certain hypotheses we choose to ignore at this moment are satisfied. I should note that the term "efficient" is used here in the very particular sense first associated with the name of the Italian economist, sociologist and philosopher, Vilfredo Pareto. Pareto held that one situation or allocation is better than another if every individual involved feels that it is better according to his own individual values. So we speak of an allocation as being efficient if there is no other allocation which is better in this sense.

The price system has additional virtues. Not only is it capable of achieving efficient allocation of resources, but it requires that the participants in the economy possess relatively little knowledge. They need only worry about their own needs and desires. Individuals in their ideal state need not concern themselves about the social effects of their actions. If one does something which affects others, for example, if one withdraws resources that others could use, he is made aware of it through the price he has to pay, and therefore he does not have to consider further the other effects and other individuals.

Despite the favorable properties of the price system, I am no unrestrained admirer of it. Some of its limits in the urban context will be stressed below. It is not possible, however, to understand the city as an economic problem without first understanding the virtues of the free market system in performing its role of allocating resources.

FREE MARKETS AND THE GROWTH OF CITIES

The historical development of cities and metropolitan areas and their growth relative to the rest of a country is in large measure the natural and beneficent result of economic forces. The essential element has been a shift in population from rural to urban areas as a result of shifting economic opportunities. The industrial and commercial activities of the cities have grown steadily. In turn, rising productivity means rising incomes. Now, it is a firmly established generalization that as income levels rise the proportion that individuals wish to spend on agricultural products directly or indirectly falls. Perhaps I should point out that given this tendency of the demand for agricultural products to rise slowly, the rising productivity in agriculture has the same effect on population movement as does rising productivity in industry. That is, if the demand for bread tends to rise relatively slowly and if less workers are needed to produce a given amount of wheat, a shift of farm laborers to the cities follows.

The mechanism which directly induces these shifts is the market through an increase in industrial wages relative to agricultural incomes and through the creation of more job opportunities in the cities. Therefore, the spectacular increase in productivity in the last two centuries resulted in the growth of cities for two reasons: first, because cities were the location of the technologically advancing industries, and second, because cities were recipients of the farm laborers rendered less important by the shift in demands to manufactured products due to rising incomes.

The economically induced shift to the cities has repeated itself wherever industrialization has occurred and under a wide variety of circumstances and institutions. English farm laborers flocked into the textile mills and the iron and steel plants in the early 19th century just as the Russian muzhiks did in the Soviet Union in the last 40 years. On a more global basis the peasants and rural villagers of Ireland and then later of southern Italy and eastern Europe followed the path of economic opportunity across the Atlantic in greater numbers and over greater distances than any other migration in human history. Most recently it has been black and white sharecroppers from the South who have left areas where their productivity was low and have gone to the cities where it is much higher.

From the economic viewpoint this movement must be judged overall a great success, exactly what theoretical defenders of the price system would have expected to happen. National income has risen precisely because each migrant moved to a situation of higher income. Remember always that income typically reflects productivity, that is, real contribution to the national income.

Suburbanization as a Result of the Price System

Let us consider another much-discussed aspect of the changing role of the city, the movement within metropolitan areas from city to suburbs. Here again, the basic motivation is found in individual preferences. In this case, though, the individuals are pursuing greater satisfaction rather than increases in productivity and income. The suburbs offer attributes desired by many if not most individuals: space, greenery, and in some cases better education and other public services. These are costly, so that suburban living is something of a luxury good. As incomes rise, more individuals can afford the luxury, and the flight to the suburbs is on. Decreases in transport costs—first through the railroad and then through the automobile—have contributed further to suburbanization.

Again, this movement in good measure conforms with the theoretical model of overall improvement due to the price system. Those who do move presumably are better off; otherwise they would not go. Those who do not move are not worse off; indeed, the movement of so many out of the city reduces the competition for urban space and keeps rents and property values below what they otherwise would be.

Nevertheless, the out-migration to the suburbs does have one consequence that some deplore. Because suburban living is to a large extent a luxury good, it is the well-to-do who move and the poor who are left behind. The result is a greater segregation by income level than probably was the case a century ago.

FAILURES OF THE PRICE SYSTEM

Let me now turn to the negative side, the failures of the price system. There are two major aspects in which the price system falls seriously short of providing an ideal allocation of resources to achieve social aims. One, to which I shall return later, is that the

distribution of income in a private enterprise system is determined
by the possession of skills and property which satisfy demands,
but without any guarantee that the resulting distribution of income
will conform to our ideas of justice.

The second failing of the system is what economists call "externalities." Essentially, externalities arise when transactions between individuals convey far more benefits to some individuals
than to others but when no price tags accompany these greater
benefits. To clarify the meaning of externality, let me give a somewhat trivial example. Two cars come to an intersection at right
angles, one perhaps slightly before the other. Let us suppose the
driver of the second car is in a great hurry, for good or bad reasons,
while the other would be only mildly disturbed by a delay. If the
first driver could sell his priority to the second driver, the second
would have to pay a price to compensate the first for his delay and
yet this price would be such that the driver in a hurry would prefer
to buy the priority rather than be late. Both would be better off
than if the first simply exercised his priority with no price tag
attached. For obvious reasons, such a price system is not practical
for operation so society substitutes inefficient but practical rules
of priority—in this instance, traffic lights.

The classic examples of externalities are public goods, those
commodities which have been found expedient to supply through
government. It is impractical or unwise to supply such services as
legal justice, police protection or fire fighting through the price
system. The essential point is that there is no way of separating
the benefits to one from benefits to others. If crime is prevented,
for example, there is no specific beneficiary whom we can ask to
pay on pain of losing his protection. There is no effective price
system; any individual can refuse to pay without losing the benefit of crime reduction. So we find it necessary to provide an
alternative means of allocating resources: the government makes
its decisions through political and administrative techniques and
appropriates the necessary resources through the tax system.

Education, by the way, provides an interesting example, as it is perfectly practical to set up a price system for education. A pupil is excluded unless he or his parents pay, just as the child is refused bread unless someone pays. Of course, this price system is used in private education. The question may be and has been raised: why should the government supply education? The usual argument is that education benefits others than the individuals who are educated. In fact, the presence of an educated citizenry is of political value, and very possibly also improves the efficiency of the economy. But this general benefit cannot be priced in the sense that any of those who receive the advantages of living in a well-educated society could be deprived of this benefit if they chose not to pay for it. Also, the values of the parent may be opposed to those of the child. The parent may prefer the child's current income to his future well-being. The child, in the absence of social, governmental controls, would have no recourse through the market. It has therefore been judged appropriate for the government not merely to supply public education, but in fact to make it compulsory.

Other externalities also are beginning to affect government policy: congestion, pollution of air and water, and in a more general sense, the quality of life. All of these, as well as the more familiar governmental functions, raise more intense problems in the cities than elsewhere. The crowding of the cities due to the scarcity of urban space multiplies the magnitude and frequency of external interactions on the individual. Further, it is possible that the congestion relaxes inhibitions against antisocial behavior. The anonymity of the large city may serve to increase aggression and alienation and thus render more intense such problems as crime.

Once a government is in existence and meets some or all of the externalities just discussed, the very existence of the government leads to further externalities. A particular government is itself only a unit in a larger system. The city is in competition with and has relations with other governmental units.

FISCAL AND DISCRIMINATORY HORRORS

The most obvious economic manifestation of the urban crisis is the fiscal problem. The ability of a municipality to meet its problems depends in the first instance on the resources it can command through the tax system. But a city with in-migration of rural poor and out-migration to the suburbs has a steadily reduced potential for meeting its problems. Indeed, there is an instability in this system. The relative decrease in the tax base leads to poor municipal services, from education to street cleaning. From the viewpoint of the well-to-do the advantages of the suburbs become even greater, increasing the out-migration and so forth in the usual cumulative process.

The horrors of racial discrimination in housing and employment compound all these problems. Racial discrimination is more effective in the suburbs, so blacks are disportionately concentrated in the central city. Then racial prejudice adds to the motives of many well-to-do whites to go to the suburbs, thereby increasing both the fiscal problem and the black concentration in the central city.

As a somewhat special feature it so happens that the productive services carried on by governments and especially by cities differ from those in the private sector of the economic system by involving a much greater utilization of labor in proportion to output. So far, at least, automation and mechanization have had limited impact on education and on police work. As the efficiency of the economy as a whole gains, wages rise relative to prices. Hence, the costs for municipal services rise more rapidly than do prices in general. Recently, in fact, they have been increasing twice as rapidly. This means that, merely to keep governmental services increasing in proportion to other goods, the fraction of resources captured in taxation will have to rise.

Fiscal problems of cities are compounded by externalities among governmental units. The dominant form of taxation in the city is the property tax, one that can easily be enforced since its object—property—cannot run away, but one which has severe limitations in terms of both efficiency and equity. Other taxes, especially income taxes, run into the problem of competition of governmental units. Individuals can leave high tax areas for low tax areas.

One of the reactions to these problems has been the growth of grants-in-aid, largely transfers of income from the federal government to state and local governments. The federal government's ability to tax widely and fairly is much greater than that of the individual city or even state. With all its imperfections (and they are many), the income tax is the best tax we have.

The relation between the federal government and the cities and states is somewhat the same as between a welfare department and its clients. That is, the federal government has taken a very paternalistic role by handing out its money for very specific purposes in the form of the so-called categorical grants. There are currently various proposals for block grants instead of grants-in-aid, calling for income transfers to the state and local governments with little if any restriction on the purposes for which the money could be used. Allocations perhaps might be simply proportional to population. This would of course increase greatly the flexibility of local government to treat their varying problems in their own ways.

Such a fiscal pattern may serve as a precedent for the introduction of a new level of government. It is too early to be sure how things will develop, but, as we all know, there is considerable pressure for the creation of smaller units within the city. School decentralization in New York may be an important beginning. Fiscal independence is difficult enough for a city, and would be a self-defeating absurdity for these smaller units. But an elaborate system of categorical grants would defeat the feeling of autonomy which is precisely the aim of decentralization.

INCOME REDISTRIBUTION AND JUSTICE

Let me return to the topic of income redistribution, which I alluded to earlier. As we have seen, the price system leads to a relatively efficient allocation of resources. But let us recall the definition of efficiency used here. An allocation is efficient if there is no other system which makes everyone better off. Efficiency in this sense is thoroughly compatible with great inequality in income. So there is no presumption that an efficient distribution of income is just. Yet there are strong moral imperatives in our culture for greater equality. Empirically, the relative inequality of income in the United States has shown some long-range tendency to reduction, but in the last twenty years it has remained unchanged. And, as we are now all aware, the inequality is indeed substantial. This is true even within the white population, though of course more pronounced between the races. No doubt our perception of this problem has been intensified by a period of affluence. The existing inequality is more easily remediable and more anomalous in these prosperous times.

Even though the issue of income distribution is not specifically an urban problem, the contrasts of wealth are felt most sharply in the cities. Indeed, the fiscal problems of the cities stem in part from the fact that they have been more responsive to the demands for justice to the poor. To cite one figure, aid for a family of four with dependent children totals $250 a month in New York City and $35 a month in Mississippi, with cost of living factors explaining only a small part of that difference. However, though the pressure on the cities to serve as agencies of redistribution is great, their ability to perform this function unaided is small.

Redistribution in its most straightforward form means taxing the rich and giving to the poor. A tax system which could do this most effectively is the income tax; yet we have already seen that it is the most difficult for the cities to use. A more successful redistribution might occur with federal aid, which may be used, for example, for ghetto jobs, housing, or other special services. But we must ask how the economic system as a whole will react to such measures. In actual fact, improving the status of the poor and the blacks in particular cities and especially in particular areas is likely to induce further in-migration and preservation of the ghetto as natural economic responses. This, of course, is not all bad. In fact in-migrants and the ghetto residents are the gainers. But it would appear even better to make redistribution a genuinely national function.

It is not more efficient for individuals to move merely because redistribution is being carried out more effectively and more extensively in the cities or in particular parts of them. Some plans for a guaranteed minimum income, sometimes called a negative income tax, and carried out by the federal government everywhere, would seem highly preferable to specific improvements in the cities, which will in the long run only add to their burdens.

To recapitulate, the present state of the cities, including their fiscal crises and their tensions, is in good measure the outcome of natural and beneficial forces in the market. The difficulties arise from the variety of resource allocation problems for which the market fails to find a solution. These problems are most intense in the cities, and that is where the demands to correct the injustices of the income distribution perpetrated by the market are also the greatest.

Politics and the city

James G. March

Urban political science is an important branch of the empirical
study of politics. Contributors to the field include not only political scientists but also political sociologists, urban anthropologists,
urban economists, and other social scientists who have observed
political man in the cities. As a result of their efforts, we know
some important things about the political structure and political
process in the city. I will not attempt to review that empirical
knowledge in any comprehensive way here. Rather, it is my inten-
tion to approach the analysis of the city from the point of view of
political theory, to consider the political process in the city as a
system for making decisions, and to assess the political position of
the city in the United States.

The strategy is simple: First, a basic model of politics is outlined
and its more conspicuous properties identified. Second, the circumstances under which such a political system will be preferred to
some other system (for example, the price system) are discussed.
Third, the theory is related to the place of the city in national and
state politics and to the urban political scene. Fourth, the apparent
implications for public policy are suggested.

A PURE THEORY OF DEMOCRACY

Consider a more or less "pure theory of democracy." It is a pure theory in that it is never achieved but serves both as a model of what a political system might be and as an approximate representation of actual politics in western democracies. Thus, we will use the theory for two classic purposes. On the one hand, we can discuss the properties of a "pure democracy" and the extent to which any particular real system approximates those properties as it approximates the assumptions underlying the theory. On the other hand, we can use the theory to predict outcomes in systems that satisfy reasonably the assumptions. The intent in focusing on a theory of democracy is not to suggest that politics in other systems is necessarily fundamentally different. It probably is not. But by limiting the focus in this way, we can exploit the very convenient political accounting procedures represented by elections and the individual vote.

In this "pure theory" we assume that each citizen casts his vote for one of a set of candidates. The candidate chosen by the largest number of voters is elected and thereby assumes all legislative and administrative power until a new election. In order to secure votes, candidates engage in various kinds of promises and other deals with voters. In the entire process each voter is assumed to be trying to maximize his net return from political involvement and decisions; each candidate is assumed to be trying to maximize his likelihood of election.

As is well known, voting systems have some important technical difficulties (for example, the voting paradox) that are bothersome; but the major difficulty is sometimes overlooked: The "pure" system implicitly assumes that the set of candidates presented to the voters represents the final step in a complex process by which all of the possible coalitions of voters and all of the possible policy proposals of candidates have, in some sense, been considered. We require assurance that when the final election is held, there is no alternative set of policy proposals (that is, candidate) that would have been successful in winning the election if it had been presented. In order to make such assurances, we require that the rewards for collusive suppression of a potentially winning set of policies are less than the rewards of victory at the polls for at least one of the necessary partners to the collusion; that the rewards for the effort of discovering and negotiating potentially winning policies are great enough to guarantee that all such policies are, in fact, discovered; and that any potentially winning set of policies will have sufficient access to the communication system to be considered actively by the voters.

It is clear from this that the theory and the system it describes depend heavily on the process by which political coalitions are formed and bargains made and enforced. In effect, we assume that politicians and public bureaucrats are continually negotiating with citizens to arrange trades. Through these trades, for example, a citizen with a special interest in clean air may join with another citizen interested in a baseball stadium to make what amounts to a contract to support each other's proposals. Such trading exploits a standard feature of all barter: the differences among citizens in personal value assigned to alternative policies (associated with different intensities of feelings felt by different citizens about the various alternatives feasible within the political system).

In the usual political democracy, these trades are arranged through party platforms and promises, through legislative deals, through administrative negotiations with clients. They are commonly called "logrolling" (or statesmanship) when they are negotiated prior to legislation and "fixing" (or flexible administration) when negotiated later. Out of the need to develop such agreements among voters come the paraphernalia of modern politics— the political party, the interest group, the lobbyist, and publicist, the political pundit, the expeditor, the Washington representative. This constitutes the indispensable institutional apparatus of the system.

The "pure" system, in effect, functions to establish an exchange procedure that combines the technical efficiency of a perfect barter system with equality of power (among voters). It does not provide the theorems of the "pure" price system concerning the relation between income and productivity; and some of the most interesting potential implications of the theory—those concerning the tradeoffs between equal voting power and the distribution of unequal productivity and wealth (the theory of bribes and political intervention in the price system)—have never been adequately developed. Nevertheless, we can attribute to the system (in its pure form) considerable social welfare "efficiency."

A political system of the sort describable in these terms has several conspicuous properties relevant to treating it as a decision-making system and particularly relevant to ways in which we think about improving public decision making. Consider the following three:

First, the political system renders decisions without achieving shared goals. We do not expect, do not require, and do not observe consistent collective goals. In this sense, a political system is more like a price system than it is like some relatively conventional views of organizations or individuals as decision makers.

Second, the political system reacts as a function of source rather than content. Whether air pollution is a "problem" depends on who thinks it is and how many potential votes he commands. As a result, the system is likely to function relatively poorly if there is a significant disconnection between the individuals affected by a decision and the effective constituency for the decision (since trading across constituency lines is comparatively difficult).

Third, the staff and analysis needs of the system are fundamentally oriented to understanding possible future citizen reactions to decisions, not other consequences. It is no accident that the social scientific analyses securing the greatest interest (that is, commanding the greatest price) from the political world are those directly concerned with voter sentiments (for example, opinion polling) or with concerns easily related by any intelligent person to voter concerns (for example, fiscal and monetary policy).

Taken collectively, these properties suggest that improvements in the political system will come about primarily through improving the capabilities of the prime actors (politicians and voters) in the system to pursue their roles intelligently and imaginatively rather than through the application of modern decision analysis to the problems of an assumed set of public objectives. The two tactics of analysis are not, of course, independent; but as long as we have major problems of "frictions" in the system, we need to devote major resources to reducing them. This point is, as we shall see, particularly compelling in urban politics.

CONDITIONS FOR USE OF A POLITICAL SYSTEM

We turn to the circumstances under which a political system might be used. There are a number of major problems in the price system (for example, externalities and income distribution) that might induce us to seek political (or other) intervention in allocation decisions. It is potentially misleading, however, to operate on an implicit assumption that the price system is the primary system and others are used where it clearly "fails." The price system and the political system are competing systems for reaching social decisions. More properly, various price systems and various political systems (including revolution) are competing. For all practical purposes any one of the systems and many combinations can be used to make the same classes of decisions (namely, who will live where, what kinds of transportation will be provided, who will have what income).

The key features of the various systems are that they do not, in general, render identical decisions and that none of their technical properties permit us unequivocally to choose one over the other. For example, the Pareto-efficiency of the price system might be cited as a basis for preferring that system. That feature of a "pure" price system assures us that there exists no alternative allocation that would be preferred by everyone to the allocation resulting from the operation of the price system. Although a plausible case might be made for Pareto-efficiency as a necessary property of a socially desirable allocation of resources, it cannot be viewed as sufficient without accepting an extraordinary bias against change.

The number of Pareto-optimal solutions to the allocation of resources in the United States is uncountably large. The solution generated by the price system is one such solution, but it is not necessarily the one that will be most preferred by every individual (or any individual). As a result, each individual in the country can be viewed as deciding what system to prefer for what purpose.

We can imagine various economic, social, political and revolutionary systems as an assortment of "games" having different rules and (typically) different outcomes. We expect each individual and group to come to prefer (either through rational calculation or learning) to have decisions made through games favorable to him. For example, within politics we expect those individuals who have a relatively favorable position in national elections (that is, cohesive and flexible groups in large states, Democrats) to espouse a political ideology of national interest and deprecate "states rights." We expect those individuals with a relatively favorable position within states (that is, white residents of the rural south, Republicans) to construct an ideology of political decentralization from the national government to the states and political centralization from the cities to the states.

Our more general question, however, is not about the preferences within politics but the choice between politics and alternative choice methods. In order to determine who might reasonably be expected to show a bias toward the political "game," we ask simply: Who does comparatively better in politics? The question deserves a more detailed answer than will be attempted here, but there are three general observations that may be worth noting:

First, although absolute advantage undoubtedly belongs to the rich and the educated in both the economic system and the political system, the *comparative* advantage of the poor and less educated appears to lie in politics. Thus, in general, so long as there are no exceptional "frictions" in politics, the political system will tend to be somewhat less biased in favor of the rich and educated than the economic system.

Second, because of some persistent problems in political adjustment between elections, the "ins" always have at least a short-run comparative advantage in politics. As a result, cries of the need to separate politics from other things (for example, business, science, education) and the ideology that "that government governs best that governs least" are conspicuously cries and ideologies of losers.

Third, the political system, like the economic system, has an "income distribution" problem. The young and the highly mobile, for example, are politically "poor." The economic power of young consumers has produced substantial effects on the goods and services offered in current markets at a time when the same group has been relatively weak in normal political activity.

It is less easy to answer the social policy question of when the political system *ought* to be used in preference to others. Such a question presumes some agreement on the goals involved in establishing the system. However, if we accept the general democratic values that underlie the "pure" democratic system, we can at least argue that a political system will generally become more attractive as it more closely approximates the assumptions underlying the pure form, that is, when the "frictions" are minimal. The "frictions," in turn, depend heavily on the quality of political negotiation within the system.

In particular, it seems clear that the amount and quality of political brokerage required by the system is a function of some fairly ordinary variables:

Size of the political unit. The greater the number of citizens, the greater the brokerage requirements. Moreover, the relation is probably not linear. Brokerage needs seem to increase a good deal faster than the number of people.

Average education and income in the unit. The more a citizen can assume his own political brokerage function, the less the need for special brokers. In general, the ability to assume such a function is related to the knowledge provided by education and the access to resources provided by income.

Amount of slack in the system. The problem of inventing new solutions that effectively maintain a political coalition are easier when resources are substantial than when they are tight. We require more brokerage time and talent in low slack times than in high slack times.

Thus, with fixed rewards for political brokerage, the political system will function better (in the sense of satisfying the expectations of the theory) in small units than in large, in high education-income areas than in low, in good times than in bad. Alternatively, we can observe that to maintain a fixed quality of the process, we must invest more in brokerage in large units than in small, more in poor-uneducated areas than in others, more in bad times than in good. Unfortunately, it appears to be true that for the most part we do precisely the opposite.

THE CITY AND POLITICS

Consider the city and politics in two ways: first, the city in the national political arena; second, the city as a political system.

Our basic democratic model seems to have some modest validity when applied to national politics in the United States. Insofar as it does, it casts some light on the difficulties urban leaders face in

entering winning national coalitions. A first straightforward prediction of the theory is that a favored coalition member will be a
group having demands that are consistent with large numbers of
other demands. (If the world consisted of three pressure groups—
business, labor, and farmers—with approximately the demands
such groups make and if any two could form a winning coalition,
we might expect farmers to win most of the time.) The major demands made by the cities do not appear to have such politically
attractive properties. In particular, they ask for massive subsidies
(that is, money) which presumably must come in large part from
personal income (through taxes), defense, or education.

A second straightforward prediction of the theory is that
leaders who cannot influence votes are not favored coalition members. As a political force, the urban ghetto vote suffers from its
relatively small size. Compared to the problems of organizing a
viable coalition, the number of potential votes in the central city
is small. It suffers additionally from the relative loyalty of urban
voters. The urban voter does not appear to be easily influenced
by governmental policy with respect to the cities. In fact, he
appears to be a relatively "captive" voter, changing allegiances
slowly.

The city also seems to suffer as a political system. On the sur-
face, urban political systems do not appear to function well. This
is true in two senses: First, the system does not seem to meet the
assumptions of the "pure theory." As a result, we cannot claim
for it the kinds of efficient democratic properties that hold for
the pure case. Second, the quality of life in the cities seems poor
and the political system seems unable to cope with that fact.

It is not obvious that improving the system as a political system would necessarily improve the "quality of life." It will do so
only if improved quality is a relatively high priority demand by
many people. Nevertheless, we can examine the failures of the
urban political system to meet the assumptions of a pure system
of parliamentary democracy as a means to understanding the

problems of urban democracy. They are substantial failures:

> Many key persons in the system are not primarily—or even sig-
> nificantly— concerned about winning reelection. Civil service
> protection for employees, the tendency for high level political
> and technical personnel to become—or anticipate becoming—
> employees elsewhere (usually with clients whom they are regu-
> lating), the tendency for urban politics to be a part-time activity,
> all of these (whatever their other merits) weaken the political
> structure of the city.
>
> For many citizens the city is a consumption or investment item
> (a product in the economic system), not a political entity. Dis-
> satisfaction leads to emigration rather than voting one's dis-
> pleasure. This is particularly true of those people—mobile, edu-
> cated middle-class—who have the highest general sense of politi-
> cal efficacy.
>
> Relatively little pressure is applied on the city political system
> to be concerned about the future consequences of current
> actions. All political systems have a disturbing bias in favor of
> the living generations. The unborn do not vote. In the city this
> bias is multiplied by mobility and lack of commitment to the
> city. As a result, we can expect a persistent inclination in all
> politics, but particularly in cities, to sacrifice long-run virtues
> to immediate exigencies.
>
> The effective constituency in a city rarely matches very well
> with the affected group. The relations between suburbs and the
> city, between visitors and residents, between state and city are
> clearly a strain on politics. A political "income distribution"
> problem arises when important affected people do not have the
> political leverage of a vote. The result is less political efficiency
> in arranging trades and a movement toward expanding the
> political unit to a larger, presumably more inclusive and cer-

tainly more ungainly, unit (for example, the involvement of the state government in "local" affairs; the movement toward "metropolitan" government).

The invention and negotiation of effective logrolls and fixes require a high level of political organization and a rich structure of political brokers. This becomes particularly critical as you drive out of the city those people who are most competent (as individuals) to function without brokerage assistance. Yet, in the modern American city, the rewards for brokers are meagre.

In politics it is tempting to emphasize a theory of choice (the voters choose candidates, and so forth) and to ignore the process by which alternatives are invented, modified, and sold; that is, political research, development, and marketing. We ignore it in the theory; and we ignore it as a necessity in the city. The primary way in which a political system can stimulate such political research, development and brokerage is through the incentives it offers to individuals in the political system. In the traditional American urban political system, graft of various sorts provided such an incentive. As a result, we quite probably had a better functioning political system in our cities 60 years ago than we do today.

Graft as a reward system had little attractiveness to most of us. It demeans the creativity it subsidizes and is almost certainly less efficient than a number of other incentive systems from the point of view of producing a smoothly functioning political system. Nevertheless, we must recognize that the elimination of graft has reduced the incentives for creative political leadership in the cities at precisely the time when the demands on that leadership have become greatest. The cities will always recruit a handful of dedicated brokers for whom internal rewards of personal satisfaction will exist regardless of the palpable refusal of the society to lend credibility to that satisfaction by external rewards of money, status, deference, and honor. A society is foolish, however, to

ignore the overwhelming evidence that talent and commitment
go where the rewards are.

IMPLICATIONS FOR PUBLIC POLICY

For all of the reasons outlined above, it seems clear that the city
is in serious political trouble. City residents have relatively little
leverage within the national political scene given the existing
political rules and given the current demands of other potential
coalition members. Significant improvement in that position
might come in any one of three major ways:

First, city residents might extract concessions by a credible
threat to abandon the existing political rules—in short, by
threatening insurrection. Second, a massive external change (for
example, a major business depression or uncontrolled inflation)
might produce a set of new demands from other coalition members that would make city residents more attractive as members
of a winning coalition. Third, anything that improved the political organization in the city—in particular the brokerage function—
would strengthen the national position of the city. Political
organization could be strengthened by reducing the degree to
which the city is a consumption item (either by reducing the
number of attractive alternatives or by decreasing the ease of
access to them). It could be strengthened by improving the incentives for multiple political brokers within the city.

Of the three major alternatives, the third seems most attractive.
Insurrection has the conspicuous disadvantage that its effectiveness requires fine calculation and control on the side of both the
revolutionaries and the state. The threat and the bribe depend on
careful calibration of the joint consequences of a "bluff" being
called. It is hard to see how such a tactic has high prospects of
success (for the city) in the absence of good political organization
at the city level. Indeed, one of the major sources of stability in a

democratic political system is the fact that, under normal circumstances, the political organization that makes insurrection feasible
also either makes it unnecessary or permits the limitation of its
use to controlled tactics of threat and bribery.

Massive economic dislocation has the disadvantage of its obvious
side effects. For example, the coalition favoring political intervention to inhibit inflation is tenuous enough to suggest that under
certain economic conditions even the modest political muscle in
the cities might be adequate to contribute decisively to inflationary governmental policies. A combination of strong economic
pressure and inflationary governmental policy has a chance of producing sufficient economic chaos to force a reorganization of
coalitions and thereby improve the position of the city residents.
Without a greater certainty that such a maneuver would succeed,
however, it seems unlikely that we (even if "we" means the city)
would choose to pay the social costs of major inflation for the un-
certain benefits of an only dimly seen political realignment.

Political organization of the cities, on the other hand, is unam-
biguously attractive. It offers to improve the position of the cities
nationally; it offers to improve the political process within the
cities. It offers the possibility of differentially improving the
quality of life for poor people. Whereas many tactics for "improving" the city operate to drive the poor from the city (by raising the
price of life in the city—for example, through urban renewal),
strengthening the democratic political process operates to make the
city differentially better for the poor. The reasons have already
been indicated above. The poor probably have a comparative advantage in politics; this advantage is substantially dissipated in
political systems that do not provide an effective political organization.

Of the two ways for strengthening political organization, the
alternative of reducing the extent to which the city is seen as a
consumption item seems more difficult. It conspicuously goes
against the main announced objective of transportation systems

(that is, moving people in and out of the cities from the suburbs). It goes against the housing aspiration patterns of mobile parts of our society (for example, the house as a temporary investment). Some help may come fortuitously through the collapse of freeway systems; or the pervasive destruction of the environment (so that the differences between the quality of the environment of Lake Forest and Chicago become essentially indistinguishable); or the slowing of growth in the economy (so that mobility of employees— through building new plants—is reduced). Each of these would help political organization through forcing a greater number of citizens to attend to the city as a community rather than a com- modity. Each, however, seems a high cost to pay.

If we are to strengthen and improve the city, therefore, we need to devise new ways to improve political brokerage within the city. If we do not subsidize political competition, the exchange of polit- ical information, and the creation of political groups, the urban political system simply will not function well. Among the major current suggestions for improving life in the cities, two will con- tribute significantly to building political organization. The first is to increase substantially the amount of resources available to the cities. The greater the stake, the greater the effort and talent it will attract. The second is to provide flexible resources to alternative, potentially competing groups in the cities. Our cities need a wider variety of more active politicians and political activists.

We need somehow, however, to go beyond these efforts to make political brokerage attractive. We need to invent some acceptable and useful ways by which imaginative and effective political leadership may be rewarded. The quality of life in a city is valuable to individual citizens. It is reflected in a low assault rate on citi- zens, in the quality of medical and social care provided to citizens, in the quality of education provided children and adults. Quality in a city is produced to a substantial degree by political-civic leader- ship, but few of the gains are returned to that leadership.

Changes in the quality of life result, for example, in increases and decreases in the price of real estate within a city; but most of those gains and losses are reaped by persons (even as you and me) whose contributions are much less than those of the political brokers. This curious situation has been recognized implicitly by land and community developers, many of whom have effectively (and successfully) become private political entrepreneurs in order to capture some share of the benefits of political leadership. Perhaps we can learn from such efforts. Perhaps we should provide political management with a share of the capital gains (and losses) in real estate. It seems reasonable to suspect that good police forces will be more common if the police force shares in the profits resulting from its services; good ward heelers will be more common if the ward heeler shares in the profits.

The linkage to real estate values is intended to be illustrative, not decisive. There are other ways to make natural links between community benefits and personal rewards for leadership. The main point is simply that such linkages would help to recruit a deep network of political leaders. The recruitment of such leaders is a necessity for rebuilding the political organization of the cities; and major improvement in organization is necessary before the political system in the cities will provide anything approximating the theoretical attractiveness of our "pure theory of democracy," and before the cities can become a more significant political force within the national political world.

The Social Basis of
Markets and Governments

James S. Coleman

There are a number of aspects of society which greatly affect the functioning of markets and the functioning of governments. I will briefly discuss several of these and then focus on one.

Professor Arrow described two ways in which the price system breaks down. One is externalities, which are costs or benefits imposed by an action of one party or by a transaction between two parties on a third party. The second is inequities of distribution.

EXTERNALITIES AND INEQUITIES

Externalities arise most often as a consequence of geographic contiguity between two parties: the contiguity between a smoke-producing factory and a residence, or between a noise-producing railroad and a school. As a consequence, the question of geographic location becomes extremely important in assessing externalities imposed by individuals on one another. This is particularly relevant to problems of urban society and problems of urban areas, because urban areas are defined by, in fact, their demographic concentra-

tion. One large study of the economics of New York City, for
example, concluded that the principal economic advantages which
kept the city alive are the external economies for newly-developing
industries created by contiguity of other resources.

This importance of contiguity makes the study of population
movements, of why people move, and of demographic concentration a very important one for the functioning of markets. Discrimination against Negroes in housing, for example, leading to
racial segregation by residence, is closely related to the problem of
externalities: most whites assume that Negroes in their neighborhood will impose external diseconomies on them, for example, in
terms of increased crime, or decreased value of property.

The second problem discussed by Professor Arrow, distributional problems deriving from the price system, is very much related to the problem of different starting points. A large compo-
nent of the distributional problem of the price system is due to the
fact that people do not begin at the same starting point. There are
several ways in which people do not begin at the same starting
point. One of these has to do with existing wealth and inheritance
of that wealth. Another, which is probably much more important
in our society, has to do with the ability to perform in the society—
ability to do things which will command value.

This problem of different starting points leads directly to the
educational system and the family as the two principal factors
affecting the starting point. The price system thus depends directly
upon a strong educational system: one which can in large part
overcome the differences in starting point imposed by the family.
If the educational system functioned well in this sense, then the
price system would function better as a mechanism for allocating
goods and services than it presently does. As a consequence, one of
the major problems in the functioning of the American economy
lies in the fact that educational institutions are not better able to
bring children with low starting points up to a level that enables

them to command values in the economic system. Research and action programs in education have made some headway in the problem, but it remains largely unsolved.

These are two ways in which other aspects of the society, demographic concentration and educational institutions, impinge upon the problems of the price system that Professor Arrow described. I will mention in addition two ways in which the institutional basis of society affects those governmental actions described by Professor March.

MAJORITIES, MINORITIES, AND SATISFACTIONS

The first of these has to do with the social basis of political cleavage. Throughout history, political cleavage in society has derived from other institutional ties among individuals. In earliest representative government, for example in early Rome, kinship was the formal basis for representation: the Roman Senate was composed of heads of family estates. In some societies even now, ethnicity is a basis for representation, and in others religion is a basis for representation. And apart from formal representation, structural aspects of society such as occupation come to constitute important bases of political cleavage, bases through which political demands are made.

Since pluralist democratic politics requires overlapping and crosscutting cleavages, this means that such a political system is viable only in certain kinds of social structures. For example, if race were the sole basis of political cleavage in a society, then a pluralist democratic system of politics would not be viable, because one race or the other would be a permanent minority, subject to the will of the majority. None of the political negotiations, vote trading, and deals through which intense minorities can realize some of their aims is possible because the minority's support is never needed.

A second way in which the society or some aspects of the society affect the functioning of the government has to do with the relation between sizes of minorities and the decision rule. A majority rule is the most frequent rule in democratic politics, but for certain actions, greater consensus, such as two-thirds, is required. Such modifications of the majority rule are designed to protect the interests of minorities, in situations when political negotiations, vote trading, and political markets are not functioning adequately. Thus in a decision that requires a two-thirds or three-fourths majority for action (as is often true for constitutional changes), a political minority of one-third or one-fourth can block action. Thus, the designers of the rules of government must take carefully into account the likelihood of intense minorities and adjust the rules so that majorities cannot always dominate minorities and minorities cannot always thwart majority action.

Now I will turn to the principal aspect of the social basis of the functioning of markets and governments that I want to discuss. This can best be introduced through five terms. The terms are *confidence, trust, legitimacy, force*, and *productivity*. The peculiar thing about the first four of these terms is that they are not called into question during most of our existence. During most of the time that a society functions, questions of confidence in the economy or in the government, questions of trust and legitimacy, and problems involving force, do not arise. It is only with the possibility of withdrawal of confidence, withdrawal of trust, withdrawal of legitimacy, and use of countervailing force that these terms become of particular interest. Recently, confidence, trust, and legitimacy have become much more problematic than they have been in a long time. For that reason it is especially useful to examine their relation to the functioning of economies and their relation to the functioning of governments. Some examples will illustrate this relation.

Confidence

The first has to do with the Weimar Republic in Germany in 1923 when confidence in the government's guarantee of the value of money was at its lowest ebb. An item that cost five million marks in the morning cost 10 million marks in the afternoon. A worker paid on Friday would distribute his wages to his children so they could spend it simultaneously, because of the rise in prices that would occur if it were spent sequentially by one person. This was a time of extreme loss of confidence in the economy, and in the government as the bank for that economy. A reverse example was France in 1968. Economists could show that the economy did not have the productivity and the possibility of exports to enable it to function without devaluation of the franc. However it was the force of de Gaulle's personality, confidence that de Gaulle would not devalue when he said he would not devalue, which stopped the selling of francs when de Gaulle refused to devalue.

These are two simple examples illustrating the importance of *confidence* in the economy and in the government's action as a bank for that economy. We might ask what are the conditions for withdrawal of confidence? The principal thing underlying the confidence itself is the economic reality, that is, the *productivity* of the economy—the economy's ability to maintain exports at least equal to imports at the given rate of international exchange. At the same time, confidence may vanish even if the economy does have that productivity. Under such conditions, no bank can stand an extended run, even if it is a government bank. Thus productivity of the economy constitutes the underlying reality that maintains stability of the price system; yet the functioning of the government as a bank is extremely dependent upon a very intangible thing which can best be described by confidence.

Trust

The second of the five terms is *trust*. Trust is closely related to confidence, but whereas confidence may be described in this context as a belief in the continued ability to perform productively, trust involves something more: it involves the belief that the other party will repay an obligation when it might be to his immediate interest to escape it.

A first example of the importance of trust is the rotating credit associations of communities in southeast Asia, described by Clifford Geertz. These associations are a combination of social activities and economic activities. One person gathers his neighbors (somewhere between 10 and 30 in number), invites them to participate in a continuing set of social occasions carried out weekly or monthly. On these occasions each person makes a contribution. The sum total of these contributions goes to one person. Geertz noted the way in which these associations have been used and are used to make capital investments which could not be made either because of the absence of saving habits or because of the absence of any kind of lending institutions at a reasonable rate of interest. Capital investments such as the purchase of a bicycle can be a very important thing in such economies.

Something like these rotating credit associations has spread rather widely. There was a recent description in the news media of something like rotating credit associations in Brazil for the purchase of automobiles. A group of men, each interested in buying an automobile, convenes each month and makes payments sufficient to purchase one automobile. The winner is determined by lot, and excluded from subsequent drawings. The group continues until each has his automobile.

This institution functions in effect to provide economic capital, for persons who have little capital and little credit with lending institutions. The importance of trust for such institutions to develop lies in the fact that one person receives money at a time which may be far later than the time at which he initially made his investment. Those who make the contributions must have a great deal of trust in the other persons, for each knows he may receive his lump sum last.

Another example of such mutual trust is in early industrial England, the industrializing period of Lancashire, in which bills of exchange were very widely used. Bills of exchange were substitutes for money, substitutes for Bank of England money and substitutes for money from local merchant banks. At that time the Lancashire industrialists had a greater degree of trust in one another than they had in the banks themselves. The bills of exchange were in effect notes from one manufacturer to a supplier of that manufacturer. The notes were successively passed on and endorsed by each of the manufacturers through whose hands they passed, and guaranteed by each of these manufacturers. Other money, banknotes from local or central bankers, was used in transactions only at a discount, relative to the bill of exchange as the prime money.

This kind of interpersonal or community trust has a direct parallel in trust of government institutions and government policy. Two examples will illustrate such trust and its withdrawal. The first is McCarthyism in the United States in the early 1950's. It is possible to look at McCarthyism as a period during which there was great withdrawal of trust from the government by many persons in the society. McCarthy in effect was beginning a withdrawal of trust by attempting to create a run on the government, by purporting to find untrustworthy actions in members of the State Department. In effect, he sponsored a run on the credit of the government.

A second example, similar in form, although responded to by a different set of persons, is now occurring with the anti-Vietnam movement in the late 1960's. In this case, intellectuals sponsored a run on the credit of the U.S. government by questioning the legitimacy of the United States' Vietnam involvement. There came to be, I think as a consequence, a withdrawal of trust by a different set of people than the people who withdrew trust during the McCarthy period, but nevertheless, a similar run on trust in the government.

Again, what are the conditions for withdrawal of trust in government? The matter is directly analogous to confidence in the economy: the economy has a certain level of productivity which satisfies individual wants, and confidence in the economy is created by its continued production of these satisfactions. Government is a system for producing collective satisfaction and the source of trust in the government is its continued production of collective satisfaction. When the government fails over a long period of time to produce such collective satisfaction, whether the failures are due to the government itself or due to the intractibility of the environment, there then tends to be a withdrawal of trust.

I suspect the situations leading to the withdrawal of trust in the two periods that I have described are quite similar. The frustrations due to the Korean War and frustrations due to the Vietnam war constitute a continued lack of generation of collective satisfaction through government policies. If the government is a system of production of collective satisfaction, then that system has not been functioning as well as it has in the past. There is a loss of trust at certain periods of time, and those periods of time are periods in which the government's level of production of collective satisfaction falls.

Legitimacy

This general way of looking at confidence and trust in the economy and the government leads directly to the third of the five terms I introduced earlier: *legitimacy*. When the members of a society have confidence in the economy and trust in the government, they are in effect making investments in the institutions of the economy and the government. When these investments are maintained over a period of time, it may be said that the members of society have accorded legitimacy to those institutions. Legitimacy is based on confidence and trust, but goes beyond them.

Force

Confidence and trust are attitudes toward the current functioning of the economy and the government; legitimacy is a general acceptance of the institution, and acceptance of the rules it implies. Withdrawal of legitimacy follows withdrawal of confidence and trust, and implies a rejection of the institution itself—for example, rejection of the economic system and the price system that regulates it, or rejection of the government institutions. Since this rejection is a rejection of the very rules under which the society functions, it ordinarily takes place only through overthrow of those rules by *force*, our fourth term. Thus force is the ultimate means by which choices in society are implemented. In the economy, choices are implemented through the use of money; in the political system, choices are implemented by casting a vote; but when the very existence of these institutions is in question, the rules themselves no longer hold, and choices are implemented by force.

Thus the price system which operates through the exercise of individual choice, and the political system which operates through the exercise of collective choice, are themselves products of a meta-choice—a choice among institutions which establish the rules. The choice is continually reaffirmed through the continued investment of confidence and trust, or weakened through withdrawal of confidence and trust.

Given this framework of ideas, let us turn to problems in urban areas involving trust in government policies and legitimacy attributed to government by subgroups in the population. When markets and individuals exercise a choice through free markets, and thereby impose external diseconomies or result in poor distribution, and when government attempts to reduce the externalities and poor distribution through some collective activities, then if there are failures in this second system of production of collective satisfaction, there is a withdrawal of trust, and in the longer range a withdrawal of legitimacy. A general example of this, illustrated by poverty policies of the past several years, is that in a democratic system advocates of redistributional policies must understate the cost and overstate the benefits in order to generate support for the policies. This creates a set of expectations with regard to costs and benefits which cannot be met. Expectations of potential beneficiaries were raised with the poverty program, but government policy was relatively ineffective in producing the benefits of redistribution.

A joint consequence of increase in expectations and the failure to meet those expectations is a withdrawal of trust in government actions and an investment of trust in actions of other groups. Black militants, the Black Panthers probably being the best example, represent such action groups in which legitimacy is invested by some Negroes as an alternative investment, once it is withdrawn from federal, state, and local governments.

Another example starts with the Civil Rights Act of 1964 and other civil rights legal and legislative action. This legislation led to an expectation by Negroes of much more civil treatment from police than had occurred in the past. Yet there were no broad administrative changes in police forces to produce a change in police actions. As a consequence, there has been a withdrawal of legitimacy, not because the police are less civil to Negroes, but because their actions have not changed as rapidly as the change in expectations. This withdrawal of legitimacy accorded to police in the black urban ghetto, is accompanied by the investment of legitimacy in black community vigilantes, acting as a countervailing force to the police.

Another kind of example which has led to the same kind of withdrawal of legitimacy or withdrawal of confidence and withdrawal of trust is the existence of increased externalities imposed by Negroes on whites in the form of crime in urban areas. This crime, relatively unchecked by government, leads to a withdrawal of confidence by whites, and in a few cases the establishment of white vigilantes.

The question that finally arises is: how is confidence, trust and legitimacy in the government and the economy restored when some withdrawal has begun, as it has begun on the part of many groups of the population at present in the United States.

Productivity

This leads to the fifth term of the five which I introduced earlier: *productivity*. Confidence in the economic system and legitimacy of its institutions is restored through the productivity of the economy for all subgroups in it, including those who are currently disadvantaged. Trust in the government, and legitimacy of the system of government is restored by the productivity of government in overcoming problems of externalities and problems of distribution, without imposing costs on others that will induce their withdrawal of confidence, trust, and legitimacy. In short, the long run means by which confidence, trust, legitimacy in government and in the economy comes to exist is through the productivity of the economy in producing individual satisfactions, and the productivity of the government in producing collective satisfaction.

The Future of
American Ghettos

Anthony Downs

My assignment is to present a practical application of the social
sciences in the formation of social policy regarding an urgent
urban problem. The problem I have chosen is the future of American ghettos. I will try to look at this problem in a way that illustrates how the principles and techniques of social science can be
concretely used to develop public policies.

APPLIED SOCIAL SCIENCE AND SOCIAL POLICIES

However, before setting forth my illustration, I wish to point out
some of the difficulties which arise in any attempt to use social
science as the foundation for practical social policies. First, real-
world problems never follow the rather rigid jurisdictional lines of
academic organization. In fact, attacking almost any social problem effectively requires the use of many different social science
specialties. But true interdisciplinary efforts in the social sciences
are quite rare. The incentive structure of the academic world
simply does not reward them very highly. Consequently, individual

practitioners like myself who are in the cruel, hard world of assist-
ing actual decision-makers are forced to use inputs from many
disciplines, as you will see.

A second problem is the astonishing lack of basic data about
real-world conditions in the social sciences. You would be amazed
if you knew how ignorant we social scientists are about many of
the basic processes which greatly influence our lives every day.
Furthermore, it is extremely difficult to make up for this lack of
information by conducting social experiments aimed at producing
proper data. Most people object to being guinea pigs, and resent
being included in anything which appears to be a "social experiment." Also, policy-makers are always under tremendous time-
pressure to "do something" immediately. Therefore, they cannot
afford to wait for lengthy experiments before taking action. Furthermore, the allocation of resources by politicians is dominated
by what I call the "Iron Law of Political Dispersion." This is a
fancy name for a congressman's saying, "If you are going to have
a costly experiment in your district, I had better get the same kind
of goodies in mine." As a result, any attempt to create an experiment in one congressional district is under great pressure to expand rapidly into a nationwide program so as to spread the benefits over a broader political base.

This is precisely what happened to many programs in the Office
of Economic Opportunity. Many of its original programs were intended as experiments to be conducted on a limited scale. Even the
entire OEO itself was supposed to be an experimental innovative
office attached to the presidency. But because of the "Iron Law"
mentioned above, OEO mushroomed into the custodian of huge
nationwide programs before any of them had been adequately
tested in a relatively small area. All of these factors mean that the
kind of experimenting which is the foundation of scientific advance
in physical and natural sciences is extremely difficult and unusual
in social sciences. The resulting lack of accurate data puts a pre-

mium on insightful judgment and the ingenious analysis of inadequate existing data.

Another important aspect of policy-formation in the social
sciences is that the skill needed to formulate workable policies is
very different from the ability to analyze the likely causes of
existing conditions. The typical academic social scientist is essentially an analyst; that is, his skill is that of breaking down complex
situations into their constituent causes. But what is required in
formulating social policy is *synthesis*; that is, the building up of
practically workable programs from fragmentary and diverse
inputs.

This is similar to the difference between basic research and
applied or developmental research. But the latter is almost non-
existent in the social sciences. Yet there is no more reason to believe that skilled analysts are also good synthesizers than there is
to believe that an excellent food chemist is necessarily an out-
standing cook. This discrepancy again puts a premium on insightful judgment and practical wisdom. Hopefully, these virtues are
based upon a strong knowledge of the findings of social science.
But they also require skills not always found in purely academic
settings, such as practical experience and common sense.

There are many other things that could be said about the pit-
falls of using social science to formulate social policies. However,
I do not have time to add to those I have already mentioned. I
have picked them out because you will see practical illustrations
of their application in the remainder of this talk.

KEY BACKGROUND FACTS FOR THE FUTURE OF GHETTOS

Since the Watts riots in 1965, the conditions in, and future of,
what have come to be called "American ghettos" have become key
national issues of vital importance. Yet there is sufficient igno-

rance about the basic realities concerned so that any analysis of this issue must begin with a clear statement of a few background facts. Then policies can be formulated and evaluated by building on these facts.

What Does "Ghetto" Mean?

The first item to be addressed is the meaning of the word "ghetto." It usually denotes compulsory living in some kind of an enclave by members of some identifiable group. However, it can be interpreted either economically or racially. The economic interpretation refers to poor people who are compelled to live together in ghettos because they cannot afford to move elsewhere. The racial interpretation refers to people of a certain racial composition who are compelled to live together in one district by outside pressures and discrimination against them. This was the case in Europe in relation to Jewish communities where the word "ghetto" was first used. I use the racial sense in talking about American ghettos.

Therefore, I define those ghettos as the entire non-white population of the central cities in our 224 metropolitan areas. Since 92 percent of all American non-whites are Negroes, data about non-whites are essentially the same as those about Negroes. This racial definition of American ghettos means that middle-income and upper-income Negroes, as well as poor ones, are included in what I have defined as ghettos.

In 1966, there were between 12 million and 14 million persons in American ghettos defined in this way. We do not know the exact total because the Census Bureau is unable to find the great many people who live in ghettos. It admittedly undercounted the Negro population in 1960 by about 10 percent in the nation as a whole. In other words, the Census Bureau could not find about two million Negroes. In Chicago, we did a very careful study of school enrollment data to check up on the accuracy of the Census

Bureau's population data. We discovered an undercount among Negroes of 16 percent, or a failure to count about 157,000 people in the city of Chicago in 1960.

But even allowing for an undercount, less than seven percent of the total U.S. population lives in ghettos as I have defined them. This means that 93 percent of the population does *not* live in ghettos. I emphasize that obvious conclusion because it is related to an important point that James March made in his talk. He pointed out that, in a nation run by majority rule, the country as a whole is not likely to worry very much about what is happening to only seven per cent of its population—at least normal political processes may not pay much attention to this group. This apathy is particularly likely because the seven percent concerned are among the lowest-income and least influential people in society.

Ghetto Population Dynamics

A second important background fact concerns the dynamics of ghetto population. We hear many people talk about how the United States must break up or disperse the ghettos, as though such actions were real possibilities. Actually, ghettos are not only failing to shrink, break up, or disperse—they are growing rapidly. From 1960 to 1966, all ghettos in the United States defined as noted above were growing in population at about 400,000 persons per year. In contrast, the number of white persons in the same central cities dropped by as much as 4.9 million from 1960 to 1966 because of massive out-migration to suburban areas. These conditions created striking disparities in the racial composition of population growth in central cities on the one hand, and suburbs on the other hand. From 1960 to 1966, over 100 percent of the net increase in the central city population was Negro, since the white population was declining. In contrast, only about two percent of the population growth in the suburbs was

Negro, whereas 98 percent of suburban population growth was white. In fact, there was actually an out-migration of Negroes from suburbs into central cities in that period. This polarization of growth rates illustrates what the Kerner Commission meant by continued movement towards two separate societies.

Since 1966, the Census Bureau has issued new data which depict trends very different from those described above. Those data indicate a marked slowdown of Negro growth in central cities, and a big increase of Negro growth in suburbs. Frankly, I do not have much confidence in the accuracy of these figures. I believe there has been a slowdown of ghetto growth, but I do not think it has been as drastic as the Census Bureau shows. Rather, it appears to me that Negro growth in most large cities is continuing except where the ghetto has spilled over into the suburbs. This does not indicate any lessening of racial segregation in housing. Rather, the segregated areas have passed over the central city limits and spilled into suburban areas, as in St. Louis. Moreover, even the Census Bureau's figures show that white out-migration from central cities is occurring faster than ever.

It is undoubtedly true that fertility and birth rates among both whites and Negroes have slowed down sharply in the past decade. Fertility rates—which indicate the number of live births per 1,000 women between the ages of 15 and 44—reached their peaks in both ethnic groups in 1957. Since then, these rates have fallen by about 30 percent. Nevertheless, the Negro fertility rate is still almost 45 percent higher than the white fertility rate. This is mainly the result of educational differences between Negroes and whites. In fact, the fertility rate among college-educated Negro women is actually lower than among college-educated white women. Nevertheless, there is still a very high birth rate in the Negro population as compared to the white population. And the main cause of ghetto growth now is natural increase within the existing ghetto population, rather than migration of more Negroes into big cities.

The "Law of Cultural Dominance"

The third background fact critical to this analysis is not really a single fact, but rather a theory of white residential behavior. This theory has been developed by my father and myself based upon our empirical observations over the years. It is admittedly not firmly-grounded in statistical analysis, since adequate data are simply not available. Nevertheless, we believe the kind of behavior depicted by this theory plays a vital role in social change in large American cities. The imprecision of our theory is typical of the way practitioners must use imperfect raw materials in trying to develop concrete policies in the social sciences.

We refer to this theory as the "Law of Cultural Dominance." In our opinion, most white families do not object to living in the same neighborhood as Negroes. In fact, we believe a vast majority of whites of all income groups would be willing to send their children to integrated schools or live in integrated neighborhoods, as long as they were sure that the white group concerned would remain in the majority in those facilities or areas. The residential and educational objectives of these whites are not dependent upon their maintaining any kind of "ethnic purity" in their neighborhoods or schools. Rather, those objectives depend on their maintaining a certain degree of "cultural dominance" therein.

These whites—like most other middleclass citizens of any race—want to be sure that the social, cultural, and economic millieu and values of their group dominate their own residential environment and the educational environment of their children. This desire in turn springs from the typical middleclass belief of all racial groups that everyday life should be primarily a *value-reinforcing* experience for both adults and children, rather than primarily a *value-altering* one. The best way to insure that this will happen is to somewhat isolate oneself and one's children in an everyday environment dominated by—but not necessarily exclusively comprised of—other families and children whose social, economic, cultural, and even religious views and attitudes are approximately the same as one's own.

There is no intrinsic reason why race or color should be perceived as a value relevant to attaining such homogeneity. Clearly, race and color have no necessary linkage with the kinds of social, cultural, economic, or religious characteristics and values that can have a true functional impact upon adults and children. Yet I believe a majority of middleclass white Americans still perceive race and color as relevant factors in their assessment of the kind of homogeneity they seek to attain. Moreover, this false perception is reinforced by their lack of everyday experience and contact with Negroes who are, in fact, like them in all important respects. Therefore, in deciding whether a given neighborhood or a given school exhibits the kind of environment in which "their own" traits are and will remain dominant, they consider Negroes as members of "another" group.

It is true that some people want themselves and their children to be immersed in a wide variety of viewpoints, values, and types of people, rather than a relatively homogeneous group. This desire is particularly strong among the intellectuals who dominate the urban planning profession. They are also the strongest supporters of big-city life and the most vitriolic critics of suburbia. Yet I believe their viewpoint—though dominant in recent public discussions of urban problems—is actually shared by only a tiny minority of Americans of any racial group.

Almost everyone favors at least some exposure to a wide variety of viewpoints. But experience in our own society and most others shows that the overwhelming majority of middleclass families choose residential locations and schools precisely in order to provide the kind of value-reinforcing experience described above. This is why most Jews live in predominantly Jewish neighborhoods, even in the suburbs; why Catholic parents continue to support separate school systems; and partly why so few middleclass Negro families have been willing to risk moving to all-white suburbs even where there is almost no threat of any kind of harassment.

I am not trying to defend the behavior described by this "Law of Cultural Dominance." Yet however demeaning this phenomenon may be to Negroes, it must be recognized if we are to understand why residential segregation has persisted so strongly in the United States, and what conditions are necessary to create successful racial integration. The growth of non-white residential areas has led to "massive transition" from white to Negro occupancy mainly because there has been no mechanism that could assure the whites in any given area that they would remain in the majority after Negroes once began entering.

Normal population turnover causes about 20 percent of the residents of the average U.S. neighborhood to move out every year. Such moves occur because of income changes, job transfers, shifts in life-cycle position, or debts. In order for a neighborhood to retain any given character, the persons who move in to occupy the resulting vacancies must be similar to those who have departed.

But once Negroes begin entering an all-white neighborhood near the ghetto, most other white families become convinced that the area will eventually become all Negro, mainly because this has happened so often before. Hence it is difficult to persuade whites not now living there to move in and occupy vacancies. They are only willing to move into neighborhoods where whites are now the dominant majority and seem likely to remain so. So the whites who would otherwise have moved in from elsewhere stop doing so. This means that almost all vacancies are eventually occupied by Negroes, and the neighborhood inexorably shifts toward a heavy Negro majority. Once this happens, the remaining whites also seek to leave. They do not wish to remain in an area where they have lost their culturally dominant position. Yet the key mechanism in this transition is not any flight from the neighborhood by the whites that were there initially. Rather it is the failure of other whites to keep moving into the neighborhood.

Thus racial transition occurs, and stable integration is prevented, because there is no mechanism by which whites can simultaneously achieve two objectives. The first is living in an integrated neighborhood so that whites and Negroes can experience living together. The second objective is living in an area in which whites remain the dominant group.

For reasons beyond the control of each individual, whites must choose between complete segregation or living in an area heavily dominated by members of what they consider "another group." Given their values, they choose the former. Thus the "Law of Cultural Dominance" is very important because it means that the growth of the Negro population in our big cities leads to more segregation and a constant expansion of the racial ghetto, rather than wider experience of racially integrated living. In my opinion, it would be highly desirable if race and color ultimately became insignificant factors in human interaction, similar to the color of one's eyes or hair. Yet it will be difficult to alter present attitudes, so that race and color really do become insignificant, if whites and Negroes do not ever have any experience in living together and discovering how similar they really are.

Thus, reducing the centrality of race and color as issues and barriers in human relations appears to require some means of allowing whites to live in integrated areas while remaining assured of dominance—at least as long as present white racial attitudes persist. One means of doing this would be the creation of integrated neighborhoods away from the ghetto, particularly in suburban areas distant from large all-Negro neighborhoods. In such areas, the appearance of a few Negro residents would not immediately herald the potential arrival of many more because of the pressure of nearby ghetto expansion. This possibility is directly relevant to one of the ghetto futures set forth later in this article.

I readily admit that this whole concept is extremely controversial and raises many difficult questions. For example, why should Negroes want to live in an integrated neighborhood if they must always be in the minority? After all, Negroes might also conceive of desirable integration as a mixture of racism in which *they* are the dominant group. However, if both whites and Negroes insist on local dominance in order to achieve integration, we will never have any integration. Unfortunately, I do not have time to discuss this emotion-laden issue any further.

The Fiscal Squeeze on City Governments

The fourth significant background fact concerns the fiscal squeeze on local and state governments. This squeeze is especially acute in older central cities where the concentration of low-income population is much greater than in newer suburbs. James March mentioned that some aims of city governments tend to drive wealthy people out of the central city. In addition, certain factors and practices in American urban areas tend to attract the poor into central cities. Those cities contain the oldest housing in metropolitan areas, since they were built first.

In the United States, the oldest housing is typically in the worst physical condition, and is, therefore, the least expensive and the most available to poor people. This is not necessarily true in many parts of the rest of the world. Particularly in relatively underdeveloped countries, the poorest people in society live in brand new housing. They build such housing themselves in the form of shacks created on the edge of each major city. However, in the United States we have such high moral principles that we impose middle-class standards on the construction of all new housing—even housing designed for lower-income occupancy. Therefore, we do not allow anyone to build a new substandard quality unit—that is, a shack. Yet many poor people can afford to live only in extremely low-quality housing. Since we prevent them from building new low-quality housing, they must make older housing low-quality enough so they can afford it. This means they must go and live in the center of our large cities where the oldest housing stock is concentrated. As a result, we have a high concentration of low-income populations, particularly recent in-migrants, in the middle of our central cities and in some older suburbs. In relatively underdeveloped countries, low-income in-migrants are concentrated on the outskirts of the cities, or scattered through them.

Moreover, our rigid political boundaries mean the central cities are fiscally isolated from the remainder of the metropolitan area. So the rising concentration of low-income residents within their boundaries creates a growing need for expenditures by those cities to serve the costly needs of poor people. At the same time, property values stagnate or even decline because those poor people cannot afford to maintain their homes in good condition, or to spend enough money to keep local stores prosperous./The resulting squeeze on central-city finances is worsened by inflation and the rising wages that Ken Arrow described in his analysis. So central-city governments—and even suburban governments—find themselves in an increasingly desperate financial position. This is extremely important in part because it reduces the willingness of middle-income citizens to engage in income redistribution, since their local property taxes are skyrocketing anyway.

Other Background Factors

There are many other background facts relevant to the future of American ghettos. These include the aging of central cities, rising incomes, and the impact of mass media on the aspirations of the poor and of minority-group members. Unfortunately, I must omit any discussion of these critical issues because of the pressures of time. Thus, I find myself in the same position as many government decision-makers dealing with urban affairs. That is, they are so hard-pressed by the pressures of time and the shortage of resources for planning that they must make decisions without any detailed analysis of some of the most important factors concerned.

ALTERNATIVE FUTURES FOR AMERICAN GHETTOS

Keeping in mind all the background facts described above, let us now consider alternative possible futures of American ghettos. In theory, we could conceive of hundreds of various futures containing different conditions. However, I believe it is useful to arbitrarily conceive of three basic alternatives in order to focus on the key choices facing society. These are similar to the three alternatives presented in chapter 16 of the Kerner Commission Report.

The Present-Policies Alternative

The first of these futures is the *present-policies alternative*. It would involve continued segregation in housing and schools, continued concentration of Negro population growth primarily in central cities instead of elsewhere, and continued failure of society to transfer any really large economic aid to the most deprived portions of central cities. Under these circumstances, many older central cities will gradually become fiscally bankrupt. They will have rising expenditure needs for their own poor populations on the one hand, and on the other a relatively declining or stagnant tax base, since many well-off residents and businesses will move to the suburbs. Already some major cities are drastically curtailing their basic services because of such a "fiscal squeeze." Youngstown, Ohio, shortened its school year; Chicago has threatened to fire thousands of teachers if it does not get major state aid for its schools; and Newark has closed its public libraries. Many other cities are letting their physical plants deteriorate and their services decline in quality.

Morover, several larger U.S. cities will become predominantly Negro in population if the trends existing from 1960 to 1966 continue. About half of the ten largest cities in the U.S. already have more than a majority of Negro students in their public elementary schools. This is a harbinger of changes yet to come, when many of these cities will become like Washington. Its total population is 65 percent Negro, and it has a public school enrollment that is 95 percent Negro. Under these circumstances, at the same time that Negro mayors rightfully assume power in these cities, the cities themselves will be in ever more desperate financial condition. Many are already

destitute, but their situation will become even worse. Hence those
Negro mayors will have to appeal to Congress for federal aid. But
by that time Congress will be far more dominated by legislators
elected from suburban districts. Under the present-policies alternative, those districts will be almost entirely white. By 1985, the
suburbs will represent about 41 percent of the nation's population,
as opposed to 33 percent in 1960. Central cities will decline from
31 percent to 27 percent. So the suburbs will be the dominant force
in Congress, and if the present-policies alternative prevails, they will
still be over 95 percent white.

Congress is already refusing to give any large amounts of money
to white central-city mayors. So what will happen when Negro
mayors ask Congress for even greater assistance? The result could
conceivably involve major frustrations, disorders in central cities,
and severe retaliation by the white community. This might in turn
lead to a serious loss of individual freedom in the United States for
all blacks and many whites. I am not saying that such a drastic outcome is a certainty, or even that the probability of its happening
under a present-policies alternative is over 50 percent. On the contrary, I believe that probability is somewhere in the 10 to 25 percent range. But even that range represents a rather frightening pros-
pect, considering the kind of risk I am talking about, and its relation
to the fundamental privileges of our free society.

The Enrichment-Only Alternative

The second basic future that our society could choose is what I call
the *enrichment-only alternative*. It would involve continued segregation and continued concentration of Negro growth in central
cities and a few older suburbs, just as in the present-policies alternative. However, the enrichment-only alternative would also include
a massive economic transfer of income to the depressed areas in
ghettos and other parts of central cities. This would occur through
various federally-supported programs in housing, income mainte-

nance, crime prevention, education, health, job-creation and training, and so forth.

In order to be effective, this alternative would have to possess several important characteristics. First, it would be quite expensive in terms of public funds. My very rough estimate is that it would require from $10 billion to $30 billion per year more than we are now spending on these kinds of activities. These numbers emphasize a crucial conclusion we all hate to face: there are no cheap solutions to basic urban or ghetto problems. Second, the enrichment-only alternative should involve private-sector action to a maximum degree. This is necessary both to enlist the imagination and energy of free enterprise, and to prevent ghettos from becoming "public reservations" completely dependent upon government activity.

However, maximum private-sector involvement would *not* reduce the need for large public expenditures. Many Americans now have an image of the private sector "rescuing" the ghetto like the white knight on TV, whose lance magically removes all deficiencies at the merest touch without any real effort. Nothing could be farther from the truth. Private firms will not attack ghetto problems without being paid large subsidies to do so. This is essential because poor ghetto residents cannot afford to pay for better living conditions themselves. We do not expect private firms to build the equipment that is taking us to the moon through their charitable contributions. Nor do we create expressways by mustering the voluntary efforts of junior executives who donate their lunch-hours to progress. Rather, we pay private firms billions of dollars in public funds to achieve such objectives. A similar expenditure will be necessary in combating ghetto problems.

A third key characteristic of the enrichment-only alternative is that it must involve far more Negro control over programs and activities in Negro areas than now exists. Fourth, it must be based upon a widespread concern about ghetto problems among all American citizens, especially members of the white suburban middle class. Their political support is critical in financing the necessary programs.

This alternative is now verbally favored by many whites as a means of "bribing" Negroes to stop agitating while remaining separated from them. It is also favored by many Negroes who want to build up Black Power, but recognize they cannot do so without white money. Yet the Kerner Commission rejected this alternative because it encourages continued development of two separate societies in America: one black and one white. The Commission believed that two separate societies cannot be made equal in nature or in opportunities for their residents. They felt that the enrichment-only alternative essentially postpones America's basic commitment to providing true equality to black citizens. Moreover, it will be much harder to realize this commitment when black ghettos are even bigger than they are today.

The Enrichment-Plus-Dispersal Alternative

The third alternative future involves what I call *enrichment-plus-dispersal*. It combines large-scale federal aid to deprived ghetto areas with policies aimed at encouraging Negroes to move into white suburban areas and whites there to accept them peacefully. There are several reasons why dispersal of at least future *increases* in Negro population throughout major metropolitan areas would be desirable. Most of the new jobs being created in society are appearing in suburban areas. So helping combat ghetto unemployment requires somehow linking up those jobs and the people in ghettos who need them. Also, if the nation really wants to expand its supply of decent low-rent housing, it must build many units of such housing on vacant land because clearance and redevelopment take too long. But where is the vacant land in our major metropolitan areas? Most of it is in the suburbs.

Even making existing suburban housing easily accessible to

Negro families would greatly expand the choice of environments available to them—at least for middle-income and upper-income Negro families. Furthermore, such families could gain better access to high-quality schools if they became dispersed throughout existing suburbs. Finally, and most important, only some form of dispersal ultimately avoids the continuance of two separate and unequal societies in the United States.

It is important to realize that *dispersal* is not the same as *integration*, even though the Kerner Commission called this alternative the "Integration Future." Dispersal of Negroes into suburban areas might result in the creation of many scattered "mini-ghettos" or "ghettolettes" or even predominantly-Negro suburbs. Yet even this development would certainly expand the choice of residential environments available to Negro families. It would also provide at least some experience for members of both races in living or going to school together—vastly more such experience than the current massing of huge numbers of Negroes in solidly black ghettos. Thus, dispersal is one way to cope with the difficulties posed by the "Law of Cultural Dominance" I described earlier. After all, it is reasonable to suppose that if American Negroes had completely free choice of where to live, they would probably distribute themselves spatially the same way that the American Jewish population has distributed itself.

Most American Jews live in clusters located in predominantly Jewish neighborhoods or suburbs. But hundreds of thousands of individual Jewish families have scattered themselves throughout predominantly gentile neighborhoods. A similar combination of clustering and scattering is what we might ultimately expect of the Negro population if dispersal continued over a long period of time.

There are not now many political forces supporting the enrichment-plus-dispersal alternative. Suburban industrialists who need workers, and white-central-city politicians who fear imminent unemployment, are about the only two groups favoring dispersal. Opposition to it has been increased by ghetto rioting and by the rise of Black Power and Black Nationalist sentiments.

Nevertheless, a start toward dispersal could be made by industrial firms working with local communities to build integrated housing and open up local real estate practices. Even if most Negroes are moved by the commendable pride of Black Nationalism to remain in central-city ghettos, it seems incredible to me that *none* of the nearly 14 million Negro residents of American ghettos will want to move to the suburbs. So a start toward dispersal is not inconsistent with rising Black Nationalism.

SOCIETY'S EXISTING CHOICE AND ITS IMPLICATIONS

What choice is American society now making among these alternatives, and what are its implications for future events and policies? It seems clear to me that society has for the moment chosen the present-policies alternative. That is, we are now doing nothing more to stop deterioration or counteract deprivation in central-city ghettos, or to encourage dispersal, than we have done in the past. This alternative was what President Nixon promised in his 1968 campaign, and it is just about what his current policies add up to. Moreover, a recent study on what has been done in the one year since the Kerner Commission Report appeared indicates that very little has been accomplished to arrest the permanent division of America into separate black and white societies.

True, the Kerner Commission Report has had a profound impact on police and national guard behavior throughout the nation. I believe this impact has both increased the effectiveness of local authorities in suppressing disorders, and drastically reduced the injuries and deaths resulting from such disorders. Yet social inaction on policies aimed at attacking the fundamental conditions in ghettos means that Negroes and other poor people in urban slums still suffer from all the ill effects of both poverty and discrimination. This is true even though middleclass Negroes are definitely benefiting from wider opportunities for employment and power than ever before.

Even though society has chosen the present-policies alternative, I believe major racial riots and disorders like those in Detroit, Newark, and Watts are probably over for the next few years. We will undoubtedly have many, many violent incidents and flare-ups in cities and on high school and college campuses. These incidents may be reported as "riots" by our inflammatory news media, but they are very unlikely to spread to the massive scale of the 1967 disorders, in my opinion. Local and state authorities now react much faster, with more force, and more decisively than they once did. Moreover, Negro ghetto residents have begun to realize that they are the ones who suffer most from the damage and destruction done in rioting. Only if current efforts to halt inflation result in high-level ghetto unemployment will there be a significant danger of incidents spreading into major riots—at least for the next two years. I realize this forecast is contrary to the often-stated view that our cities are in grave danger of "blowing up" or "burning down" at any minute. Yet I believe the latter view is grossly exaggerated.

A second consequence of society's choice of the present-policies alternative—and of other forces that would exist anyway—will be rising Black Nationalism among Negroes. Insofar as Black Nationalism means great pride in being black and in the virtues and historical contributions of Negroes in America and the world, we should all commend and encourage it. But the success of Black Nationalism in really solving ghetto problems will be frustrated by the lack of money and other resources in black communities. The inherent poverty of the ghetto community means Black Nationalism cannot cope with that community's deficiencies without massive funding from whites. Failure to obtain such funding may lead to a few more incidents of despair, such as the suicidal "shoot-

out" in Cleveland last year. However, any such psychological fore-
casts are admittedly hazardous, especially when made by a white
man.

A third consequence of the present-policies alternative is that
many major urban subsidies will continue to benefit middle-income
and upper-income households rather than the poor. Unfortunately,
most Americans—especially the households who benefit—fail to
recognize these subsidies for what they really are. For example,
every American homeowner who deducts his local property taxes
and the interest on his mortgage from his federally-taxable income
is receiving a housing subsidy. The higher his income, the greater
the tax saving from these deductions. Consequently, this subsidy
primarily benefits the wealthy and many poor people do not gain
anything from it. Either they are not homeowners, or their incomes
are not high enough so that deductions provide significant tax
savings.

Today we hear a great deal of discussion about a federally-sub-
sidized family allowance for the poor. In fact, another deduction
from federally-taxable income—the $600-per-person exemption—
already constitutes a kind of family allowance. Again, the biggest
dollar benefit in tax savings from this allowance goes to the well-
off because they are in the higher tax brackets. Still another hid-
den subsidy arises from our construction of urban expressways.
These expensive roads mainly benefit relatively well-off suburban
commuters and downtown property owners. At the same time,
they impose high moving and other displacement costs on poor
slum residents whose houses are destroyed by roadway construction.

Thus, contrary to popular conceptions, our society does not oppose subsidizing individual households. We only oppose subsidizing those who need it most, in contrast to those who are relatively
well-off! As one wit has said, we believe in socialism for the rich,
and free enterprise for the poor. This policy extends to many other
areas, such as farm subsidies (which go mainly to very large and

wealthy farmers), research and testing subsidies to drug firms (which have extremely high profit ratios) and oil depletion allowances. I realize that we also provide many direct transfer payments to low-income families, such as social security and welfare. Nevertheless, our present policies support a network of subsidies which have far different effects from those normally associated with the word *subsidy* by the average citizen.

There is another consequence of the present-policies choice: the substitution of rhetorical change for real change. True progress concerning any major urban problem requires both serious institutional change, and large expenditures. Real progress is thus very expensive in terms of both money and power. Our leaders—supported by the majority of the people—do not at present want to pay these real costs. As a result, they are unable to tackle basic urban problems effectively. But they are unwilling to admit this; so they substitute the instantaneous mythical change of rhetoric for the costly institutional changes involved in real progress. Consequently, in urban affairs, leaders in both political parties and in the private sector continually rely on words instead of deeds, and make rhetorical promises as though they were carrying out actual solutions. So we hear many stirring but essentially empty slogans like "Black Capitalism," the "intervention of the private sector," and "the importance of voluntary effort."

As a social scientist, I am bound to point out that this rhetorical approach to change has a doubly deceitful effect. On the one hand, it falsely assuages the well-off. They are eager to believe that these serious problems are being adequately treated without major costs to themselves. Therefore, they are happy if they hear supposed solutions discussed so often it appears that they must actually be occurring, since this enables them to evade paying the serious costs of real progress. On the other hand, purely rhetorical change eventually disillusions the disadvantaged even more than they are now. At first, their aspirations become stimulated by public promises. But the ultimate failure of the government to deliver in accordance with its promises further reduces their faith and the credibility of the government—and the credibility of society and authority in general. The resulting sense of cynicism and rejection of basic social institutions is of critical importance to the future of our society. This corrosive attitude is not only affecting the poor, but also our own children and young people, who feel the idealism is being betrayed by false rhetoric. The result is a serious decline in the basic trust and feeling of governmental legitimacy required to hold any society together, as James Coleman previously pointed out.

True, actually carrying out major institutional changes also creates problems, tensions, and stress. In fact, that is why we have avoided trying to make many key social changes. So I am not suggesting that futures other than the present-policies alternative represent easy solutions either. But at least they do not suffer from the corrosive hypocrisy of such policies as the 1968 Housing Act. It promised to build 26 million new units in the next decade, and yet provided grossly inadequate funds for fulfillment of that promise. And it is only one of the many recent cases of the social disease of simultaneous over-commitment and under-delivery.

CONCLUSIONS

My last remarks may seem to embody too many explicit value judgments to remain in the realm of applied social science. This merely emphasizes what I believe is a crucial aspect of trying to use social science to develop social policy. In any formulation of policy alternatives, it is impossible to fully separate value judgments and intuitive elements from "purely scientific" facts and relationships. Nevertheless, I believe a careful, thorough, and responsible use of social science findings and theories can tremendously improve the quality of policy formation in both the public and private sectors. A key advantage of using social science in this way is the resulting ability to show people what values their policy choices really serve, as opposed to the values they believe those choices are serving. Thus, social science as applied to social policy can help force us to confront the logical consequences of our actions—or our failures to act—as a part of our making key decisions. I believe this is far better than acting in ignorance and just "hoping for the best," or assuming that good will somehow always produces good results in the end.

Perhaps we social scientists cannot predict the consequences of social policies with anywhere near the reliability of physical scientists predicting the outcomes of physical acts. Yet we can surely do so with far more reliability than merely trusting to chance or fate. Moreover, the best checks on our reliability consist of both open competition among ideas—which is the basic rationale for freedom of speech—and careful evaluation of policy results. Both these checks require *more* applications of social science to policy formation, by more people with more different skills, rather than less.

As a so-called urban expert, I am the first to admit that no man can say with assurance what the future of American ghettos will be. Yet by using the kind of analysis I have set forth today, I hope we can improve that future greatly, for it will greatly affect the future of our entire society.

Discussion:

Human Capabilities and Incentives

Mr. Gorham: We have a few minutes for questions. You may address any of the speakers.

Professor W. Shockley (Alexander M. Poniatoff Professor of Engineering Science, Stanford Electronics Laboratory): What about the inherited aspects of intelligence and possible racial differences? I have not heard the words inheritability or genetics mentioned. Are our urban problems associated with a disgenic explosion? That is the opposite of eugenics and means downbreeding . . . What I feel has been neglected is what might be called the human quality input to urban structure. Two examples. The percentage of nonwhite illegitimate births has approximately tripled in the past twelve years and is now increasing so as to double in another six years. In fifty years the average Negro IQ may have dropped about five points relative to that of whites, quite possibly due to the unwitting encouragement that our well-intentioned social system may give to the least able to have high birth rates.

Here is my question. Do any of the speakers have an evaluation of the relative importance of the role of human genetic potential in the change in urban problems compared to those factors discussed? Is a disgenic explosion a major factor?

Mr. Downs: As to the capabilities of the nonwhite population, in my judgment there is inadequate evidence to make a conclusion. I am not a geneticist, so I do not pose as an expert, but the evidence I have seen does not lead me to conclude that Negroes are inherently inferior or superior. If we take basketball teams, they look pretty superior. Maybe IQ tests show some contrary evidence, but these are not conclusive to me because IQ does not separate environmental from hereditary factors.

But let's assume for the moment that your hypothesis is correct, that there is some genetic difference between the Negro and White populations. If so, I do not think that it is demonstrable that this has been the key factor, or even a major one, in the change in urban problems.

The migration of Negroes to the cities is quite small compared to earlier migrations of other groups to the United States from Europe. The total migration of Negroes from south to north was about a million and a half in their decade of biggest migration, during the late 40's and the early 50's. Compare that with a decade when at least eight million people came from Europe and settled mostly in the cities. So in terms of infiltrating cities with large numbers of low-income people with a different culture, the Negro migration has not been unusual.

Neither do I think a high birth rate has been unique to any one group of migrants or that a high birth rate among Negroes necessarily has anything to do with what is worrying most people about the cities.

Mr. Lyman D. Wilbur (Chairman of the Board, International Engineering Company, San Francisco, California): I have a two-part question for Professor Arrow, who indicated that one solution to our problems is the redistribution of wealth to those of lower income. First, what do you think about the effect of getting something for nothing on the development of the attitudes and spirit of our people? Second, wouldn't it be better to spend the same amount of money—I would even say without limit—on the education of the underprivileged in order to put them in shape so they really could compete?

Mr. Arrow: That raises a very interesting issue, but before answering your questions specifically I should say that the primary idea behind redistribution of wealth is not that it is a solution, but that it is a moral imperative—that, *per se*, we want wealth to be more justly distributed than it is today. That, of course, is a value judgment.

How do you account for the fact that some do better—often enormously better—than others? The usual answers are that some people do things which are socially more desirable, that they are more capable, that they work harder, or that they are more productive. Yet we know that a great deal of the inequality in income results from differences which are hard to square with any definition of justice. Inherited wealth and, more than that, inherited attitudes, environmental factors, and (more disputable as a value judgment) inherent differences in ability are not particularly good moral criteria for differences in wealth.

The question you raised, however, is a basic one. For you may accept the points I made but still maintain that there is a problem of incentives; that is, if people are given a free ride, they will not work as hard. Well, over the last 20 or 30 years we have had a large program to subsidize farmers, but this has rarely been objected to on the grounds you mentioned. Maybe it should have been. There have been many large subsidy programs, as Mr. Downs noted, in our history. The railroads are a marvelous example. Subsidies to the oil industry in the form of the depletion allowance are usually defended on the ground that they increase the ability of the oil companies to survive; the argument that the subsidy makes oil men fat and lazy, which would be the inference in your question, is not heard.

No, I would say that the present welfare systems are ideally designed to reduce incentives, much more so than any of the alternative proposals that I very briefly canvassed. By setting an income floor, however imperfect and irregular, we actually do not tolerate extremes of poverty today, at least not in the more advanced parts of the country. Until very recent legislation, a person received x dollars to raise his income to the floor—to a decent subsistence level. But if he or she earned anything, that amount typically was deducted from the welfare payment provided by the state. In other words, we imposed in effect a 100 percent tax on the marginal dollar earned by the individual.

In contrast, the recent proposals that have been made run along the lines of assuring everybody a flat sum, and the amounts involved, by the way, are not beyond the realm of possibility. They are talking about a figure of $2,000 or $2,500 a year for a family of four. I find it a little hard to consider this a strong negative incentive.

Furthermore, under the new proposals, there is a considerable incentive to earn because the individual would be taxed at some moderate rate—say 30 to 40 percent—on the additional dollars earned. These incentives are very high, as high as they are for the better-off classes in our society.

Getting to the other part of your question, the effect of the home environment in which children are brought up will still be considerable, whatever the form or amount of income supplement. The disabilities of the parents—psychological, sociological, physical or whatever—may create an unstable sort of background. So it is obviously very attractive to discuss a positive increase in education expenditures as an alternative to our welfare system. But what is somewhat disquieting to find out is that apparently we do not know very well how to spend the money to buy the results you want. This is a factual issue, not a matter of principle. There is considerable evidence, gathered by Professor Coleman and others, that a simple increase in the resources devoted to a studentat least at the kind of moderate levels that are considered possible—does not do much if anything to increase his performance.

This may be, as frequently observed, because the extremely early periods of life set the formative stages for learning, receptivity and ability to get along, and because the social and environmental conditions have an influence over and above the resources spent. The classroom itself is a part of the social environment, and there is some evidence that integrated classes, for example, do better than segregated classes. So what I am saying is that to use education for the purposes you suggest may not be possible until we get better evidence of what will work. This will require a type of research, with various factors controlled, that for obvious reasons will be very difficult to carry out.

Mr. Gorham: I want to thank all of the speakers and participants.

We have tried to convey that the three social science disciplines have important insights to help us understand and deal with the complexity of our urban problems. The economists, political scientist and sociologist also revealed something important as they wandered in a disciplined way across each other's territory: that is, we need the help not only of the social science specialists but also of those with a broad perspective so that we can begin to see our cities whole.

7 .U73

ocesses as viewed by the
sciences / <by> Kenneth
w <and others>.